COME HERE TO THIS GATE

Rory Waterman was born in Belfast in 1981, and grew up in Lincolnshire. He lives in Nottingham. *Come Here to This Gate* is his fourth collection of poems.

CARCANET POETRY

RORY WATERMAN

COME HERE TO THIS GATE

First published in Great Britain in 2024 by
Carcanet
Alliance House, 30 Cross Street
Manchester, M 2 7AQ
www.carcanet.co.uk

A CIP catalogue record for this book is
available from the British Library.

ISBN 978 1 80017 396 5

Book design by Andrew Latimer, Carcanet
Typesetting by LiteBook Prepress Services
Printed in Great Britain by SRP Ltd, Exeter, Devon

The publisher acknowledges financial
assistance from Arts Council England.

CONTENTS

III

LINCOLNSHIRE FOLK TALES

COME HERE TO THIS GATE

AINNS WORLD OF MINIATURE MARVELS

I wanted to make the short trek up Wonmisan
and rake my eyes across a miniature Seoul
to the east, its millions hidden in concrete cubes
pressed between islands of scrub – and, deep in its bowl

of ridges, Bucheon, a circuit board live in low sun.
But the forecast threatened an 90% chance of sleet
so I'm being a Titan of tired and tiny landmarks:
mildewed Twin Towers, a ten-foot-long Downing Street,

under a dry sky of greys, sad patches of blue.
That leaf could be Larry the Cat, the whine of the kid
beside me could be… Never mind. Could I rebuild home,
check in on the woman I love, nine hours back, in bed;

or see what's become of my father, still waiting for love,
dreaming his way to the life he never made
then waking to hours of pining to go back to bed
then dreaming his way to the life he never made?

If we could still talk, Dad, I'd call, ask: do you remember
that day we took a taxi at 8 a.m.
to the foot of Mount Brandon, rose through waves of rain
a few hundred yards, gave up, came down again,

and waited like trolls beneath a metal bridge
while sheep went off around us? What else to do
all day until our driver would trundle back
with his microclimate? Then everything changed hue

so, slowly, we made it, past false peaks and mist filigree,
though I was eleven and you were, by then, nearly blind.
And gulping at gale on the summit, I showed you our bay,
sweeping a finger along the shrunken shore

to our pro tem home, too small for you to find.

2020

I.

ALL BUT FORGOTTEN

December 2020—January 2022

Loved. You can't use it in the past tense.
Ken Kesey

The past, like a severed limb, tried to fix itself onto the body of the present.
Hisham Matar

PRELUDE

I see him rounding the hairpin to Spring Hill,
whiskey legs slow down the tightest coil of pavement,
pipe clamped in smiled-thin lips, my hand in his —

the hand that prodded his a month ago,
that couldn't uncoil the fingers now pared to ash
and boxed in my boot, with nowhere else to go.

But still we dawdle down Spring Hill, don't we?
Me tethering him those final yards, knowing
none of what a toddler can't know, and happy.

1985 / 2022

I. THE SHORTEST DAY, INTWOOD WARD

She walks me briskly past a row of 'bays':
alcoves in which a body lies contorted
in each peaceable corner. Out here is chaos.
We stop at bay 5 – 'You'll know which one he is' –
then she gestures, smiles, pads off somewhere else.

And do I? Then I do. 'Hi Dad', I say,
so he judders, heaves his chin up from his chest,
beams. 'Hello, son!' His face is not quite his.
'They've still not bloody told me why I'm here...'
(They have.) I find a chair, pull up to him,

and we settle. His nappy fills beneath the blanket
as he talks about school, the 'miracle' of my birth –
the flowers on the wasteland of his life
bursting into a meadow of his making,
which we both lie in together, finally –

and this is dignity. Opposite, Brian
talks himself to sleep, snores, wakes, and talks
himself to sleep, snores, wakes, and talks, and sleeps,
his life a tight loop, easy enough to ignore,
unlike the doctor's call, now a fugue in my head:

'Sorry, but yes.' […] 'Months.' […] It's hard to say
when he'll develop symptoms.' I've looked them up,
seen clots in clotted colons, morphine drips,
taut mouths in final circles. 'What's the date?'
'The twenty-first, Dad.' 'Just another day here.'

Then he chuckles, tells me something else I recall
differently. 'Dad?' 'Yes?' 'I'm proud of you.'
He grins. It fades. Does he know that can't be true?

II. ALCOHOLIC DEMENTIA

The sheep-tracks of your mind were worn to trenches.
You said what I'd said simply didn't make sense
then blathered again about little Dietrich Pegler,
the Nazi boy at school. One of your legs
protruded, limp, from the standard-issue blanket
as you laughed a tabescent laugh, then went blank
and slept. Something beeped. Someone coughed.
The rising, falling, rising of your breath
seemed eternal labour. Your gut gurgled –
the newer you might've laughed. And soon you heard
me shift my chair – 'Hm?' – then were herded away
again. How can I, with nothing good to say
to the man you've been, become more than a carer
to what you've turned yourself into, half there?

Then what you've turned yourself into – half there
on one side of a final single bed
you might not leave till the rest of you has left –
starts, stares through me, says 'I'm being held
against my will!', tells a nurse to 'Just fuck off'
then thanks her. Old boy, when did you get like this?
The sheep-tracks of my mind are worn to trenches.
A no-man's land lies open on the bed
with nothing left to stop me crossing it,
so I do, and rub your shoulder. 'Hm?', you say,
as I retreat – happier that way.

III. TWIN OAKS NURSING HOME

Then they moved you to a home
that still wasn't home. 'Why

am I in this fucking place?
Nothing's wrong with me.'

So I'd tell you all over again,
but only the easy part ('You're

not remembering things well
at present.' 'Yes I fucking am')

and you relearned that you'd
never learn – mindless torture,

until I stopped it. Your
silences were trains departing.

But there were better times.
When? I must remember.

Some days we'd laugh then
you'd be cut off by yourself,

but still, we'd laughed ourselves
raw, and I'd been the child again,

as you'd wanted, forcing
myself into mind, weaving

in and out of your grasp. At
once. 'You're a good lad, son.'

'Do you think, Dad?' 'Yes.
What? I don't remember.'

And there was no pressure
to repay what I couldn't.

INTERLUDE: FIRST NIGHT, LINCOLN
1983

The kids on the street are glad to see the wain
but his mammy can't stop today, and she's sorry.
She wheels him out of Lower Captain Street,
across the Bann, to a bus across Coleraine,

and all of Antrim. Then high across the sea
they go, then across the waist of England
to Nanny's house, the first place he'll remember.
(You'll smash her teeth for that.) You don't know three

has now become just you, that they're not out
for the day, that when you return from Anchor Bar
her side of the bed will be colder even than usual,
his cot an empty cage. They've not gone far,

you'll reason, when you lurch in, slap the light
to find the old familiar absence there
then check the wardrobe – still full of her things –
and sneer. And then the telephone will ring.

IV. A NEAR-CIRCLE OF CADAES ON NOT GETTING LIVE-IN CARE

'It's my house—'
No—
'and they can't stop—'

you—

'me going to it!'
gave it to your wife. She says she won't—
'Why are—'
accept a live-in nurse—

'you hostile towards—'

in her house.
'her? She's not harmed you.'
No, right, she hasn't. I'm sorry.
A truce. Silence metastasising.
'What are we talking about?'

*

And if you're—
'Fuck—'
Resistant, they—

'off!'

won't believe that you'd—
'I'll smash their fucking teeth down their throats—'
accept—
'if they try to touch me!'

live-in carers, Dad.

'But I will!'
So don't threaten them.
'But I'm talking to you, aren't I?'
I hear a nurse grind his door ajar.
'What are we talking about?'

*

'I'll just walk
I'll
I'll just walk out

I'll

I'll just walk out of
I'll just walk out of here and go home
but I
but I don't have my clothes

and I don't have your

and I don't
and I don't have your
and I don't have your car.' An ice-
cream-van Ode to Joy seeps through the line,
fades. 'It's my house. What are we…'.

V. AIR THAT KILLS

On better days, I'd test what you could recall:
'Tell me about the time when…'. Off you'd go,
bounding over sun-and-sepia-soaked
conquered hills. But today? You'd never know.

The days you said you'd been 'thinking', it was harder
to make you speak. 'What were you thinking?' 'Nothing',
and maybe you didn't remember, and maybe my guesses
equalled yours. But days you said you'd been thinking,

the dead and dying air rang in our ears.
I might hear a nurse check in, a bus wheeze past,
or the startled dotard next door shouting 'OUT!'
then 'OUT!' through the walls, until that went, at last.

VI. REVERDIE

*Where had Daddy miraculously reappeared from? One could see him trying
to figure it out. I asked if I could take you outside this time. 'No, I won't allow
that', said his mother. I remained unruffled. We had a length of corridor to
play along – and improvised toys from office stuff, a desk, chairs. We looked out
at our forbidden outside world. One day, my little love, we will re-enter our
promised land.*

Andrew Waterman's 'Rory Journal', 6 March 1984

Snowdrops. Ramsons. Then visits are on again:
I set out weekly for meetings you never recall,
foot down through dewy suburbs and east towards
a great red sun blowing out above the Fens,
and reach you after breakfast – a sippy-cup
of coffee by you, or Rich Tea in your hand –

excited, though you can never understand
how I am suddenly here. The Social Services
visiting room was like this one, wasn't it?
We'd play between the kitchenette, flowers, chipboard,
all ninety minutes of access. And, being two,
I was the one thing you'd looked forward to

since last time, though I'd needed to relearn you
were Daddy. And yes, keep talking, keep talking: let's
set wind-up seals flap-flapping round the sink
and make the corridor our racetrack and
do pop-up books and cars, over and over
in talk, while that stays watermarked in your brain.

INTERLUDE: FIRST NIGHT, NORWICH
1986

Your best – only – friend knows you well
enough to hide his decanter; adults talk,
the record player tinkles Pachelbel,
'Canon and Gigue', as you pace out of time,

fumbling to find it. Soon, I'm sent to bed,
and hear you through the floor, sprat out of water
yet in your element, until each guest
has gone to a rarefied home. And then your head

appears at the door a moment, and I pretend
to snore until the check is done, then wallow
in the homely tang of Daddy's night-time breath
which stays with me. It's good. I know tomorrow

we'll romp and run until I'm taken home,
then I'll wail and fire my impotent little fists
against my mother as she pulls me close,
run for teddy, and curl up by the phone.

VII. BEING PRESENT

Not every night, but most, when I call,
and you haven't remembered what we've talked about,
I go on loop to see the half-hour out:
'So, did you listen to the footy?' 'No' –
surprise in your voice – 'no, somehow I forgot.'
'What's been on the radio? What was dinner?'
You rarely know the answers. Or the questions.
Or that you've known the things that keep you there.

But lacking heart, or having one, or both,
I keep to tiny talk – or tinier talk:
the sound of breath, yours chafing against mine,
until 'I'm tired now, son. Good night.' Tomorrow,
Dad, we'll do this again for the first time.
It won't grow old. It won't have even begun.

VIII. HOME

T-shirt weather today: a bumble bee bumps
the window, and the door of the visiting room
yawns and nudges a pot. We could go out,
sniff freedom over the fence. You'd rather not.

'You've come to take me home?' No, Dad. I've come
to bring it to you, blind on your piss-proof seat
on wheels, most of you a line of little knots
beneath a blanket. Stop-gap Clov to your Hamm –

you'd get that, and it wouldn't help – I ask
someone to bring your sippy cup, some biscuits,
and you chew them in the back of your open mouth
in quiet, 'thinking', too afraid to talk.

So I watch the ridge of your forehead, feel my own –
for impulse, or connection, which doesn't come
until a nurse does, panting, to the door,
to tell us darlings we have five minutes more.

IX. DEPRIVATION OF LIBERTY SAFEGUARD

The longest day. The day your best friend is buried.
These solemn heads are fewer than he deserves,
and numerous; his widow smiles and cries,
routine and unique; and there's a space on my pew:
your wife didn't want you here. So, I think of you,

straggled across that bed (some buttered toast
untouched beside you, perhaps, as it was this morning)
a mile away, gasping at fumes of a faith
or pining to be senseless? I don't know.
You buried alive as high sun fills the window.

INTERLUDE: FIRST NIGHT, COLERAINE
1991

A happy drunkard, when you got your way –
until, mid-laugh, her palm across your glass,
she'd dared to say she thought you'd had enough.
That one had guts. 'Your son's on holiday',

she whispered. And when she'd left, gulping tears,
we ate alone together. And was it that
I didn't speak, or was it that eight years
since I'd last been here, nothing much had changed

apart from me, now old enough to know –
but anyway, you threatened me to bed
then followed up and wobbled in the door,
shadow father. And so much stayed unsaid:

we only had a week, and she came back
next morning, Portrush beach wasn't far,
and my arm fitted neatly into yours
that evening, as we entered Anchor Bar.

X. ALL I'VE DONE FOR WANT OF WIT TO MEMORY NOW I CAN'T RECALL

You're tired again. There's nothing to talk about.
Your nos and yeses are barbed, to make that clear.
But you're scared to be alone. I help us out:

     'It's bedtime. I should go.'

Then I sing 'Good night, and joy be with you all':
'The Parting Glass' – designed to pull you near,
to make you Irish Daddy and make me small.

     It doesn't take with you, so

I hum it. We hum together through the night
by satellite, ear to mouth, mouth to ear,
then I ring off, and someone tugs your light.

XI. ON MUTE

'You misremember' became 'I don't remember',
then 'Hm', then silence. I filled it. '[…]' 'Hm.' '[…]' 'Hm.'
And that was you for now: a low-decibel him
without the I. And we rang off, but didn't.
You couldn't remember how, just let the handset
rest against you – they'd told me how you'd hide it
('bless him') under the pillow. I loitered on mute,
listened to your breath, your breath, your breath,
the silent afterwards, the life to come.

XII. PRIVATE CEREMONY

Last week, you were a baby in the corner
    of a naked room
you'd never recognised, and looked through
    the mattress, looked through me,
saw nothing you would ever recognise.
    I fucked off when you said to.
      'Okay, Dad. Bye.'

'The coroner's not come yet. I'll take you up.'
    She smiles. We walk. 'He's here.'
You are not there, and yet you are completed:
    every you you were.
'Night then, Dad', all *I*s pronounce, at once,
    and I close my eyes like yours,
      turn, leave us there.

CODA

I never told you this, but I recorded
every 'conversation', from when they called
to when they called. The thirty times you laughed
were cropped and saved on file – and the five
when I was 'son'. But much of what you'd had
was lost in rage – no good for the sound album:
each morning of waiting for my 'How are you?'
another chance to repeat 'This isn't life.
Get me home.' '[...]' 'Why not?' '[...]' 'You'll make me ill
if you don't get me home!' What else could you say?
But as you weakened, I was company,
and so were you. Your little mouthpiece breath
like sea on radio. Or shell to ear:
released, pressed, released. Then swept away.

II.

COME HERE TO THIS GATE

COME HERE TO THIS GATE

Ciaran Doyle, inside his curfewed estate,
throws chunks of brick at Brits in armoured cars.
What else is he supposed to do? One dinks
pathetic against a Hotspur, its pillar-box eyes
sliding fast up Lecky Road. Across

the border, Günter Wetzel drives slowly
to Peter Strelzyk. They plan; six months later,
they're in an attic sewing rolls of taffeta
into a bag the size of a Plattenbau,
plotting launch sites, then telling the kids. Across

the border, Afaf Odeh cuddles the child
she got to keep, wraps and pins her scarf
behind the canvas of the home they've had
for sixteen months, and lobs a rubber ball.
The lad laughs, toddles after it. Across

the border, Eva García gets her brother:
those gringos are doing drills again. So they run
to watch through mesh, holding a kicking mutt
that growls like a turbine as shields, boots, batons
edge close, edge closer, threaten no-one. Across

the border, Ho Sun-hui, a proud guide,
perhaps – but who could know? – translates the soldier
who then, purse-lipped, leads his group of tourists
to see the enemy. They wince and pick
us out, and we stare back, across the border.

THE BURR

for Togara Muzanenhamo
and my mother

I leave for my mother's, fleet through ghost suburbs and into
my plotted and pieced homeland. 'When will this bloody thing end?'
she says, gesturing a happy hug across her yard – then 'Let's go!'
and I follow her command, her boots, round the fields, the bends
in countless hedges, on a route she's treaded daily, from budding
hawthorn to bulging haws, stopping to 'gosh!' at anything

that scuttles, or to lift her binoculars, often frantically missing
whatever it was: a kestrel trembling on cloud, a green woodpecker
fanning back to its copse. She wants to show me something.
This is why I am here: love without touch, to risk her health for
our health. The hay is baled, our calves pimpled with burrs.
And, worlds away, riots are breaking out again, I tell her,

slipping my bastard phone away, sorry, as silently we decide
not to navigate what we think, even for one another. We're
in oak-stubbled parkland now, then near a stable, derelict beside
a brick-strewn, dimpled lawn where a country house stood. 'Not far'
she says, proud, then grabs for my hand as she misjudges
a stile, retracts in a blink, tumbles hard to the mud.

But she rights herself quietly, still fit enough, and on we go. And
we are not to talk about it, I know that. But eventually she talks
around it: 'I'm getting old now. I want to enjoy life while I can' –
and is this it? – as she leads me along a fence by a wood. We walk
in single file through threadbare nettles, to where an unclipped strand
of fence wire bellies towards the turf. She doesn't try for my hand

this time – and makes it. The treetops ride the breeze a little
but everything is stillness down here. A shotgun cartridge cracks
beneath her toe, a blackbird hops from a stump to scuff leaflitter.
She peers long-range like a squirrel, grass-stained little back
to me, then points: 'This way'. And as we go, I tell her about you,
that we wrote something together: she always likes to know what I do,

so let's try that. 'Zimbabwe! What's it like there?' she says, placing
'there' in a mental map of a continent she's traversed much more
extensively than I have, but I know what she means. We face
sculpted rock I recognise from childhood, that we must have come for,
but I won't tell her I've been here. 'Few cases anywhere until June. Parts
are now on the usual curve.' I cast a stone. It sails like a line on a chart.

Soon, we frown into the puzzle of a limestone lime-green fountain:
a lead pipe stub in its bowl, a handful of dirt. Ivy skeins follow
its contours still. And, over there, the old rope swing. I'll ride it again –
but who is this now, emerging from the leaf-waving shadows?
'Are you lost? This is private' he says, pointing at the new farmhouse
we'd hardly noticed: bright brick over privet. Stiffly, he guides us out.

As we march home, I check my phone again, see your email.
Harare's a ghost town, I tell her. Patrolled. Silent. Under curfew.
Shouldn't I have known? But our news is our news. America's is as well.
On my landing page this morning: another daubed, dented statue.
Crowds facing off somewhere. Burned lots. BLM/Back the Blue.
All foreign round here. A kestrel twitches, dips behind some bales –

too quick. Then we're back. She gestures another hug. I gesture one too,
and slip into gear and out of her little lane, checking for her arm
in the mirror, lifting mine, sighing. Hoping to have done no harm.

2020

LOCKDOWN MAN

You're learning Spanish and tell me that it's easy.
It doesn't sound easy, and barely sounds like Spanish.
And then you take a live-streamed yoga class:
your left foot scribbles circles in the air
because Marie in Shoreditch tells it to.
And yes, I know I'm not inclined to be fair
this afternoon, but you haven't noticed me
thank Christ, so now I'll find some shorts and vanish
for my sanctioned daily trot across our grass,
our lifeless little road, and out of view

down lifeless little roads then back to you,
pink-faced in pink nylons, clutching a glass,
greased and gulping air like a landed fish.
And soon your MacBook blares 'Experts agree
we're *near* the peak'. Why are you with me there?
You sigh, then tut, then tell me what to do:
'Wash your *hands*'. Like God, it's anywhere,
this thing, yet probably isn't. Come here, be crass,
time's wingéd chariot…. You laugh: 'You wish!'
I'm learning you. You show me that it's easy.

2020

STUDENT CUTS

Ah, this must be the place! I thought,
skidding up on my mountain bike
at 'A. J. MOODY, CH ROPIDIST'
above the door of a side-street semi.
    It didn't look much like

I'd thought it would. But anyway,
the woman on the phone seemed nice,
reassuring. I dismounted,
ambled up the weedy drive,
    knocked twice then stepped away

and smiled at Mrs Moody's smile,
which coaxed me through. 'You're somewhat late –
I'll fit you in'. I nodded, sat
at her command. My boot came off.
    'Yep, I'll handle that'

she said, like a mechanic, as
my big toe pulsed, its red bulge raw
in feeling air. 'You might want this.'
She handed me a rough pink towel.
    'What – what's it for?'

'To bite, love.' Metal clinked. A drawer
was opened, shut. I leapt up like
a startled hare and lolloped out –
relieved of two crisp twenties, sure,
    but... oh, and of my bike.

MORALITY PLAY

Again, he leaves her little flat in town
and motors up the boulevard at midnight,
never lonelier, through rows of plane trees,
their heavy lower leaves full of streetlight
and roiling overhead. Then, home, his key
stutters through the lock, nudges the door
ajar – and there's a note: 'I've let you down.
I've left. We can't go through this anymore'.

It's six months since he told Jo he's 'not happy' –
not meaning it, or knowing what he meant –
as she sunk to his chest, apologised
for all the times she hadn't thought misspent,
that they had not misspent. Christ, the surprise:
to find your life now governed by an action
you'd never thought to take. And silently,
he'd smelled her, thought of chemical reactions…

His phone lights up three times: 'I feel alone';
'You werent yrself tonite babe what was wrong?';
'Well be together soon'. He runs upstairs:
Jo's toothbrush isn't there, her rucksack's gone,
but nothing else has changed. Some of her hairs
strew her pillow. Where *is* she? Her mum's,
he thinks, then calls. It rings to answerphone.

So he texts a quick reply: 'Babe, can I come…?'

RETURN

The house fly hitting windows in your house,
then gone and lost in a dying tree
that drops a nut; the mouse
that chews, then flees;
the louse   it brushes against your books that night, sets free
with crumbs of eggs; the day you'll comb
your child's head – oh – and see
her scalp their home
of plenty;   your coupe back from a wash, plated chrome
shining where you hit that grouse;
the wall-clock's metronome;
the summerhouse
you own,   for now, your late-returning, distant spouse…

...*13 Years Ago*

Four lads around a Singer table,
four pints and mouths, one Jenga tower
tipping, your free palm flexed mid-prayer.
Of course, your – our joint – willpower
didn't stay it. And I write 'you',
elegy's convention, sour
with all you've missed these past five years:
each clatter of sticks, each happy hour.

...*11 Years Ago*

Us waving, on sand – but where? I scour
my memory. We wince, and wear
cagoules, smile from tight hoods. It's dour,
Dad, that mess of sea, sand, air!
You're blind now, and your mind's a shower
of splintered glass I can't repair –
best not to ask you during my hour-
long care home visit. You couldn't care.

...*9 Years Ago*

And there she is, trapped mid-laugh –
that 'tease me!' laugh – and pleading stare.
Her raised hand's blurred, a glob of spit
is on her lip, grass through her hair,
and she is mine and I am hers
eternally in that small square.
No. Touch the little X again.
Forget that we were ever there.

ANNIVERSARY

distantly after Andrew Marvell

Chinese lanterns! Five dull lights –
a dotted line across the dark –
that pulsed and dipped and lost its flight
piece by piece, in Belton Park.

You caught a shooting star, and poked
at where it was. Too late. We sat
in camping chairs, ineffably yoked,
sipping wine, and watched a bat

wheel out and back. Glow-worms pulsed
between the logs. Grasses frisked.
Perfect. You wanted nothing else.
I wasn't ready to take the risk.

GOOSEBERRIES
i.m.

She bends back over the bush,
pursed hand biting for curvature
among the green, and rains
three more to the tub at her feet.

Then she finds a last one, hunches,
lifts and rattles her find, is gone
inside. A tractor's been pacing
the field next door all morning,
towards, back, towards, back.
She went unnoticed, unnoticing.

And we'll have gooseberry tart –
as tart as her love, its stout fruit
as coarse and hard to sense, when
hidden and wasting in its thicket.

PERENNIALS

Wild garlic after sudden rain
that left as suddenly –
each curlicue sunlit again –
was part of all that kept her lonely:

they'd noticed it, like everything,
every spring. *The first
year alone, surely, you'd think,
would be hardest, worst.*

It's not, she said. I felt her shoulder.
We walked back to our cars,
hugged. She left. I glanced back over
their million stars.

THIS REALM, THIS ENGLAND
distantly after Walter de la Mare

He sparks the flint – his face and hands flare amber –
and grins. The isled flame judders in freezing air.
He dabs it gently to the moistened jamb.
'Shhhh!' it sighs, and takes. We leave it there

and when we come past later in the morning
the rafters are charred stumps, the walls are bare,
and neighbours gather, pointing, by police tape,
and we nudge to it, as close as we dare.

But nearby, nested halfway up a fir,
blinking, turning, and though we're not aware
of it yet, a camera in a dome
reflects our will, then watches us rush home.

ROUTINES

'Our children won't ever be accepted as Koreans',
says Jane. 'That's why we might not stay much longer.
It doesn't matter how well you speak the language:
if you don't *look* Korean' – she waves a hand round her face –

'you're not.' They've got one child, a cutesy blonde squiggle
of massive darting eyes and burpy pukey dribbles,
safe in her playpen jail, patting a plastic mobile
that jingles, jingles, jingles. 'But Jon couldn't get

a job as a prof in the States, so maybe this is us.
And it's good here.' She pauses, then makes the boast
affirming this life: 'Check out our view!' Six floors
below, a highway plays its reel of cars,

and opposite, other storage units of employees
rise from an erstwhile breeding ground for waders,
now pushed north. We're all playing life in defence;
they want their folks in Phoenix to envy this Phoenix.

'And I'm not sure we'd fit in back home these days',
she adds, to test my complicity. 'Coffee?' That
sounds good. 'Honey?' – Honey turns from the cot,
stands – 'Does this say "decaf"?' The baby giggles.

DELAYED POSTSCRIPT TO TEENAGE HEARTBREAK
for Francesca, and for Chris

We paced the grounds of a country house
   under a featureless sky
as stark trees bled out with morning rain
   and what light there was started to die,

and every time you grabbed at my hand
   I felt a little thrill
too small to warrant mention, then.
   I'm eager to feel it still –

I spent half a life being bad at that.
   And here we were, noses to wind,
simply happy, which no-one is,
   but as close as I'll ever find.

And in came her message. Later that night
   I looked at it, then at her profile:
smiley-faced. Husband gone. Two gorgeous kids.
   Was thinking of you! Been a while…

I'm planning a trip. You were so good at that –
   That's why, I guess. You okay? xxx
What would you do? I tapped out *Hello! x*
   and wasn't sure what else to say

so we messaged for hours, saying every last nothing.
   Her latest one waits in my phone,
unread and pointless. I wish her the best,
   I promise. I'm sad she's alone

and claiming to like it. I'm glad she's still there
    where little came right, nor would,
in the sprawl of a village she's never left,
    but which still makes her happy. I could

have stayed there too, raising bunnies (she loves them),
    and learned a local trade.
And I probably *would've* stayed, too. Christ!
    I probably would've stayed…

FIRST-TIME BUYERS

She dings the bell, a muffled chime
from the gut of number twenty-nine,
and both of us step off the step,
survey. This place was quite a schlep
from where we parked behind the bar
we'd called 'our future local.' Ha!
A couple emerges, whips past, and
a suited lad is left; one hand
grips an iPad, the other keys.
He holds a smile, says 'This way, please'
and leads us down a mildewed hall.
She mutters 'I think we've seen it all'
but, being English, we poke about.
Two more stand ready as we file out.

Two more stand ready as we file through
the gate of number fifty-two
which backs against the prison. Wire
coils above the back yard, higher
than anything the listing caught
on film somehow, it seems. Abort!
We curse another not-a-chance,
then curse another not-a-chance
at forty-six. And thirty-three.
It's disappointing. But stick with me:
let's find a place we want to make
a home in, for each other's sake,
perhaps. The dice are loaded, cast.
Do both show matching sides, at last?

AT A FRIEND'S SECOND WEDDING

I've known his mother best.
    She settles beside me,
rests a blotted hand across her chest,
    and isn't sure what to say –

    that's obvious.
I sense her pacemaker tapping
to go out, as it has for thirty years.
    (That, we'll learn, will happen

    with Co-op Funeralcare
    in ninety-seven days.)
Her lobes shake as she turns to me. Stares.
    'My husband?', she says,

    then blanks. Screws her mouth shut.
    Turns back. Her eyes
are a tape that won't record, that only plays
    for ninety-seven more days.

THE STEPFATHERS

'Be silent, love.' And so she was, or tried.

The drive to school was quieter than normal.
'Be good', he, said, and kissed her head, then she
ran gangly through the playground to the sandpit,
still backpacked. Little hermit crab! He left

and panic took him to church, to cross himself.
Not again tonight. And she'll forget.

Again, she tried. Until the day her sister
stopped by, unexpected, decades later,

said 'I have something serious to ask...'
Oh, it came out of them then alright,
like twine pulled from a gut into a ball
then swallowed: there's no better option now

he's only kept alive on mother's wall.

DOUBLES AT THE TENNIS CLUB

I'm sitting out this round, pretending to watch
as the rest of the second team practices for a match
at Ulverthorpe or Culverthorpe or somewhere.
Their chic cars glint by a hedge, where sparrows flood

out then in. Men stoop in studied formation.
A serve slaps a tramline. A second makes a safe arc
then *toc!* goes the ball, and the fat lad across the net
lags behind it, gives up as it splashes the fence.

He's a dad, and a lawyer or something. He must get paid
six figures. He's set the wife up with a cake shop,
or so he's said. Queen shimmers from the windows
of his Audi each time he creeps it up to the clubhouse

and 'Hi John!', someone will beam. 'Hi Dan, Geoff, Pat!',
though he just nods at me: we haven't been introduced yet.
But on court he's grease and grunts, aware and wary.
We're both at home there. And now he's calling for me.

MY FRIENDS THE COMMUNISTS

i. Loughborough

Timmy pedals his trike about the lawn
with all his tiny might, tips in a bed
of roses. Mummy's up before the lad
has registered the shock, and here it is,
but there she is. Excited, Leon yawns
and wags his tail – thump-thump – then rests his head
back across his paws. But where is dad?
Ah! Here he comes, with beers, buns, sausages.
He grinds the drum grill open, twists a knob,
and flamelets pucker. 'You want one of these?'
He holds a can – I nod – then sits a while,
then passes it. 'Congrats, mate, on the job.'
He means that. Deckchairs ripple in the breeze,
then mummy fills one, waves to Timmy, smiles.

ii. Berat

An old man sips pastis with Ismail Kadare
in... Paris, right? Some panelled brasserie.
'Yes, all those things', says Mirel. 'The other man, this' –
he prods, wobbles the frame, and steadies it –
'he is my father. The picture was taken the day
they met again in 1993,
the first time in twelve years. My father missed
my childhood: he said we'd too little to eat,
someone informed, and then... .' He locks my gaze
which drags free, flits across his little shop
of sloughed off heirlooms: old coins, chairs, a chest,
uniforms, tobacco tins and trays
from some lost workshop, and – I pick it up –
the Enver bust I'll buy my friends, in jest.

'Keep the reunified Korea in your heart'
an old man had said, palming his chest. And
okay, I do. And there it stays, doing nothing

as flight KE 907 to London lifts
from a (re)claimed island, over (re)claimed islands
stacked with containers: a concreted sarcophagus,

the memorial to Operation Chromite,
which has no other memorial. A child beside me
pulls down her mask, is chastened, frumps.

'We're progress', he had added. See it down there,
a phosphoresced capital washing round its hills,
a land of neon chaebols and kimchi jars

where new friends complete the circuits
of their lives for Samsung, Lotte, Hyundai,
as I complete this circuit for Hanjin.

See the sea ooze the yellow they don't call it
here – there – with silt from China, as we skirt
North Korean airspace. *This land is your land*

I hum before noticing. Far towns are like colonies
of barnacles; dark fishing vessels ply
what looks turbid. And when we start to cross

the safety of China, from where this – that –
is ordained, a city (Shenyang?) shifts,
a molten web in new night. Now there will be

nothing but black, the dark familiar nowhere,
and then the grind of lowering, the misted plots
of ruined nametagged earth around our lives.

III.
LINCOLNSHIRE FOLK TALES

I plodded round Chambers' Farm Wood, on the edge
    of a clay-clodded field full of wheat.
The breeze stroked it this way and that, like a hand,
    and the trees shaded me from the heat

of that hushed August day. Oh God, I loved summer,
    but not what it meant I must do:
a farm-hand's life's back-aching toil after back-
    aching toil, all summer day through,

then again, then again. So, rather than cut
    through the wood on my way to the farm,
I was traipsing along with the poppies and hares
    for five minutes, and doing no harm

till I heard a small whine, like a baby that's starting
    to blub, then to cry, then to bawl –
which it did, sure enough. So I climbed through the hedge,
    but I could find nothing at all.

Where is it? *Whose* is it? It must be that Sarah's,
    that sultry lass at number two
who used to spend time with the vicar, but now
    spends most of it drinking Bols Blue –

she must've come down here and left the poor brat,
    I thought. I was wrong. 'Gerrit off',
wheezed a tiny gruff voice. 'Gerrit off! Gerrit off!
    Gerrit off! Gerrit off! Gerrit off!'

'Get *what* off, and off *what*?' I said. Then I saw it:
    a small pair of yellow-brown feet
wearing mud boots, then a small mustard head,
    and a rock where the two bits must meet,

so I heaved the rock up in my calloused hands, threw it
    into the brambles, looked down,
and gawped as the fellow jumped up to the height
    of my knees, shouting 'Yallery Brown

is back! You've helped me more than you know,
    my lad!' His beard jinked about
like a coil of wet rope, his muddy mud head
    was all wrinkles, and small eyes peeped out,

then darted around, then settled on me.
    'You're a good lad, young Will. Don't be frit.
I know all your dreams involve women and sloth:
    I know you. Say one wish. I'll grant it.'

Now, what would you make of this odd little boggart?
    He looked like a gremlin in shrinkwrap,
a Soviet doll left behind at Chernobyl,
    a garden gnome slathered in crap,

and I wished I'd just taken the quick route to work,
    and I wished that it hadn't been me
who'd found him – and maybe I wished that he'd died,
    but he looked quite sincere. In fact, he

repeated his promise then smiled through his beard
    with a skewed grid of yellow-brown teeth
A combine spewed wheat-dust out three fields away.
    Then he said, 'What you let out beneath

that tombstone, my lad, you can't understand,
    and whether you take it or leave it,
that much will stay true. But think: your poor hands' –
    he wank-waved my way – 'they are yet

to have some time off. I could give you a wife
    who will love you, somehow. Or your job:
it could all do itself while you sit in the grass,
    or stay home and twiddle your knob.

Just say which you want.' It was tempting. I mulled:
    love? There's enough time for love
to sort itself out, so I thought (I was young),
    but no work to do? Lord above!

Maybe I'll go home and surf the net
    for ladies, or go down the pub
and she will be waiting for me, so I thought.
    'Work, please.' He nodded, then rubbed

his billiard-ball belly, then nodded again.
    'It's granted!' 'Well, thank you', I said,
though not with conviction. He flew in a rage.
    'You *must* never thank me! No shred

of a thank you I'll hear, you grateful young sod!'
    He was flailing and gritting his teeth
and pounding the clods with his clod-coloured boots.
    'Okay!' I cried. Then, with relief,

I saw he was turning to trog on his way,
    and he bounded from molehill to molehill,
but his voice carried back, bringing with it a laugh:
    'Just call when you need me, young Will:

I'm Yallery Brown. Say my name, and I'll come.
    But' – and at this, he looked back –
'don't thank me again, or I'll leave you for good.'
    Then the sprightly sprite danced up the track

and out of my life. I stood rubbing my eyes.
    What was *that*? Then I rubbed them again:
my combine was working with nobody in it –
    the chute filled the bucket with grain

as it wobbled on past. I jumped through the hedge
    and stood in a field of fresh stubs
where the wheat had all been. Then I tested my luck:
    I walked back to the village, and pub,

and it was a good afternoon. The next day
    I took the short cut to the farm
but got there a few minutes late, and my combine
    was driving itself like a charm,

then it happened again the next day. Then the next
    I just stayed at home and hid,
and the next I forgot, and lounged round the house.
    Then the phone rang. My boss. He was livid.

'Where have you been, you lazy young bastard?
    You're fired if you don't get here *now*!'
'But my work's all been done!' I said proudly. 'Well, someone
    has done it! A self-milking cow

I never did see', he stormed, 'nor a combine
    that harvests the grain on its own,
though I'm docking the wages of anyone who
    has covered your arse.' Then the phone

went dead, so I dressed, and I ran through the wood,
    hollering 'Yallery Brown!'
and he skipped out the brush and into my path.
    I slipped to a standstill, looked down,

and brandished my fist (he winked, knowingly)
    and yelped. 'What have you started?'
I blurted. 'I want my job back! I'll work hard!
    Stop doing my work!' The sprite farted

and giggled his mischievous way, and glared up.
    'Be careful this time what you say.'
He morris danced round me, trumping in step.
    'Give me my work back. Today',

I pleaded. He stopped. 'It's granted.' 'Oh, thank you!'
    I cried out, and sank to the grass,
and at what point I knew my mistake I can't say –
    was it as he thumped my arse

and kicked at my knees, and squealed 'I warned you!
    You'll see me no more! Amen!',
or was it as 'thank you' hurled out my mouth
    and couldn't be sucked in again?

But he's not been seen since, or at least not by me.
    The farm's doing well, so I hear,
though I'm not allowed back. I watch Jeremy Kyle
    on repeat, have two sprogs, and drink beer,

and tell folk the things I've been telling you now.
    And if you see Yallery Brown
leave him to die, don't ever say thank you,
    run, then find lodgings in town.

THE METHERINGHAM LASS

She's calm, but she's been crying: doglegs
    shimmer on her cheeks.
I offer the joint again. She shakes
    her head. She's cute, but reeks

of lavender and engine oil,
    and what's she doing here?
'What you doing here?', I say.
    She taps the dashboard. 'Here?

Well, I wait for someone to blunder down
    this back road late at night.
I like a boy who's on his tod,
    gripping the steering wheel tight,

scared already. That's when I act.
    It's strange here: most who pass
look scared. This is a narrow road
    but the verge we're on's not grass:

this was a runway for bombers once.'
    She gestures a pale white hand
along the moonlit, cat-eyed lane,
    which forms a sequinned band

dead straight above a rubbled concrete
    strip five times as wide.
I nod in recognition, as fields
    of maize nod either side:

the wind's picked up. 'We'd been to a dance
    near the aerodrome:
Jack had just flown his final mission.
    He said he'd take me home

on his Triumph, down the main road there.'
    She points. Headlights pass
half a mile and world away.
    'People go too fast

that way, but sometimes I find folk here.
    I've seen you a lot. That's why
I thought I'd take a punt on you,
    pop over and say hi.

In truth, I don't see many others.'
    I nod. Toke. Stub. This lane
leads nowhere but the river after
    miles of houseless fen,

and I only come to smoke some weed
    and look up at the stars
and rev my Subaru a bit,
    away from Ma and Pa.

'But when I do, and if they look
    just right, I might appear
and flail and jump to flag them down
    and scream *My boyfriend's near,*

he's hurt himself. I think it's bad.
    We were on his motorbike
and lost control. Please help me! Then
    I vanish by that dyke,

and slip back to the ether, leaving
    the smell of rotting meat.'
I turn to her – but there's nothing there,
    just some Rizlas on her seat.

THE LINCOLN IMP

The Devil was bored in his burrow one day
    and, wanting to watch a farce,
he swallowed an imp and blew him to England,
    out through the Devil's Arse

(that's a cave, look it up), then he sat back and watched
    while the imp surveyed all England's North.
'It's quite knackered already', he thought. 'What to do?'
    But he still gave it all he was worth.

First he chopped down some trees for a railway line
    but made sure the line never came,
then he raced coast to coast ripping down a Red Wall,
    then he touched all the moors with a flame,

then he cursed half the factories – those that were left –
    in Billingham, Barnsley, Bolton,
and places like that, until they shut down,
    then he made sure the Tories still won.

And he saw what he'd made and he saw it was good,
    but he wanted to see somewhere pretty,
so a Devil-sent wind sped him down to the Minster
    at Lincoln. 'Now, wait here for me',

he said to the wind as he hopped in a gutter
    somewhere above the south aisle,
then he swung through a window, perched on a cross
    and gazed down the nave for a while.

He couldn't see any old men of the cloth
  but the tills at the front were all ringing,
and tourists were frowning and pointing at stuff.
  Then some kids in the choir started singing

so he covered his ears and whipped through a door
  to the cloister, straight into a gran
who trudged through the caff there, teapot and cakes
  in her blobby little hands,

so he cursed them to taste like old boot-soles and dishcloths
  and made all the prices go up
well beyond reason, then snuck to her table
  and widdled a bit in her cup.

Then he flew through the church – up the transept, the nave –
  and swooped to the shop. It was frightening:
a thousand or more resin models of him
  glared from shelves, so he left quick as lightning

and soared to a perch at the back of the church
  to ponder a while on his own,
but an angel was trying to kip on the altar,
  saw him, and turned him to stone.

And there he still stands, holding his leg
  and grinning (an imp, when in thought,
will do that). Beelzebub took his loss well:
  he went to the Minster shop, bought

a few hundred more, dressed like a Yank tourist,
  then stopped for three cakes and a brew.
And the wind is still waiting there, robbing folk's hats,
  their scarves, their wits, and their screw.

NANNY RUTT

Math Wood is a small plot of trees south of Bourne,
    next to McDonald's and Lidl.
It's privately owned, full of shot-gun shells, pheasants –
    but still, a bit of an idyll,

and Mike lived in Bourne, and Doreen in Northorpe,
    a hamlet just south of the wood,
and Mike had got married, and Doreen had too,
    and because they were up to no good

they'd meet now and then by the well in the middle,
    kiss, fumble, roll on the loam
for a bit, then rush back for vigorous showers
    before their spouses got home

from work (someone has to). Now, Math Wood's well named.
    It's a puzzle, a subset of signs:
square roots, infinities, integers, means,
    and fives, sixes, sevens, eights, nines

weaving about on top of a congruence –
    all very pretty when light
is streaking through leaves into leaves and leaf-litter.
    It's rather less pretty at night,

but as Doreen set out, the sun splashed each tree,
    and blackberries brushed every track,
and squirrels and blackbirds were bobbing about,
    and she didn't think once to head back

till she saw a strange woman reading a book
    (*The Tenant of Wildfell Hall*)
on a log by the scraggle of path. She was filthy,
    her face obscured by a shawl,

and she didn't look up, just twisted her neck
    to the spot where Doreen now stood,
deciding to turn or to pass. Then she rasped:
    'I've seen you here, up to no good.

That fat little goon gave the clap to his wife,
    and you think you're the one, but you're not.
You'll ruin your life.' She cackled. 'Take care.'
    Was she mad? Her breath smelled like rot,

and a bottle of Buckfast was wedged in her lap.
    Yes. Doreen shot, like a rabbit,
round the foul thing, then a bend, then another,
    then she tired, decided to sit

and thumbed Mike a message: 'eva met the old hag? x'.
    'wot? x'. 'nevamind its not good x' –
then her battery died as she went to hit send.
    Shit. So she sped through the wood

for a few minutes more, and came to the well,
    but Mike hadn't made it there yet.
And half an hour later he still hadn't come.
    It wasn't like Mike to forget:

this was too new. But soon the wood changed,
    the sky going orange then black,
as bats replaced birds and the moon floated in.
    She gave up and resolved to head back.

And was it her tears, the sting of rejection,
    the dark, or blind fear she'd get caught
if Steve came home early? Whatever it was,
    her route was an infinite nought,

or something like that. Then she stopped for a rest
    by a little hut covered in ivy.
What on earth was it? She'd not been this way.
    Then a shaky voice cried 'Come to me!'

and she saw the old hag slide out from the door,
    the tattered shawl down by her waist,
her arms thrust in front as she ran straight at Doreen,
    synapses pulling her face

to a scowl of disdain. That's the last Doreen saw.
    And no, this tale has no redemption.
For that, blame the people of Northorpe or Bourne.
    (If you like it, give Rory a mention.)

YOUR SOLITARY BEECH
for my mother

You'd often walk two miles to where it wheeled
above the corn, or clods, and what appealed
were waving whips through which your gaze might drown,
those huge scars were that broken bough had healed.

To think: it was much the same when you were a girl.
To think: you were that little girl.

Alas, it was such a long way from town,
that nobody cared when they cut it down
and left it piled in a neighbouring field,
leaves going brown in a rhombus of brown.

ENVOI

I tried to open your gate. It was huge,
an oblong snug in the wall, covered in curls
and blisters of thick green paint, and creaked a bit

but wouldn't budge from its cradle of alder trunks.
Ivy tendrils and leaves hid any view
beyond the slats and bars. I pulled them aside

and that is when I saw you, the ghost of you,
twenty or so, on a splendid little lawn,
laughing with an airman, and beautiful,

and not knowing I'd ever come this way,
that I'd ever exist, not wanting me to.
You've told me this, and who am I to argue?

I stepped back, unseen, leaving you in peace,
and called you, fifty-five years later: there's no
time but the present, no other life for us

to cling to. You were out, and didn't answer,
but called me back when I was about to go.

ACKNOWLEDGEMENTS

Some of these poems, or versions of them, have previously appeared in *Agenda*, *Bad Lilies*, *Companion of His Thoughts More Green: Quatercentenary Poems for Andrew Marvell* (Broken Sleep, 2022), *The Dark Horse*, *The Friday Poem*, *The High Window*, *The Lincoln Review*, *The New Welsh Review*, *The North*, *PN Review*, *Poetry and Covid-19* (Shearsman, 2021), *Poetry Birmingham*, *Poetry London*, *The Spectator*, *Stand*, *The Times Literary Supplement*, *We're All In It Together* (Grist, 2022), and *Wild Court*.

I am grateful to Bucheon UNESCO City of Literature for awarding me a writing residency in 2020, and particularly to Jung Seoyoung, Lee Sunmin, and You Seongjun. I am also grateful to those who commented on parts of the typescript in preparation (especially Nicholas Friedman, Anjna Chouhan, Rebecca Watts, Alan Jenkins and William Ivory), to the editors and guest editors of the publications listed above, and to Michael Schmidt and John McAuliffe, my editors at Carcanet, whose faith I hope to have repaid.

And to Francesca Hardy: thank you for too many things to count.

ALL BUT FORGOTTEN
This sequence is in memory of my father, 1940—2022, It is also written in gratitude to the staff at Twin Oaks Nursing Home, Norwich.

THE BURR
This is adapted from my portion of a collaboration with Togara Muzanenhamo, without whom it would not have been possible. The original was published as 'Burrs' in *Poets Respond to Covid-19: An Anthology of Contemporary International and Collaborative Poetry* (Shearsman, 2021), which I co-edited with Anthony Caleshu. Muzanenhamo's style is largely responsible for my own in this poem: he established the loose form we adopted for the original.

COME HERE TO THIS GATE
The title quotes Ronald Reagan's propagandistic Berlin Wall Speech at the Brandenberg Gate, 12 June 1987. All people in the poem are real, though some names have been changed. The last stanza cannot entirely be true, though: tourists in North Korea and South Korea are never permitted to see one another in the Joint Security Area.

ICN TO LHR
Chaebols are South Korean-owned industrial conglomerates. They include Hanjin, founded at the end of the Second World War, which owns Korean Air. The Yellow Sea – always called the West Sea when named in English in South Korea – carries vast quantities of sand and silt.

FOUR LINCOLNSHIRE FOLK TALES

These poems keep the simple frame of an original story, but embellish the particulars. Some names and circumstances have been changed to implicate the innocent; I thank Mike, Steve, Doreen, William, Sarah, Emrys and Francis for the inspiration. The original source for 'Yallery Brown', written in Lincolnshire dialect, was collected by Marie Clothilde Balfour in 'Legends of the Carrs', *Folklore* 2.3 (1891), and was translated into standard English first by Joseph Jacobs in *More English Fairy Tales* (1894) and, more recently, by Maureen James in *Lincolnshire Folk Tales* (History Press, 2013), among others. The regular anecdotal version of 'The Metheringham Lass', and the former RAF Metheringham where it is set, are both very local to where I grew up, and the story primarily exists orally in memorates, as does the story of Nanny Rutt. 'The Lincoln Imp' concerns a grotesque in Lincoln Cathedral, the subject of one of Lincoln's most famous legends. H. J. Kesson's 1904 version, *The Legend of the Lincoln Imp*, is the oldest extant rendering of this presumably much older tale, and was published in a new edition by Ruddocks in 2019. The Cathedral shop and café were relocated in 2020, and the events recounted in my poem predate that development. I am grateful to the Arts and Humanities Research Council for funding my project 'Lincolnshire Folk Tales', which was inspired by writing these poems.